17 Controversial Truths We Choose to Ignore

Understand Our Brutal Reality and Anything is Possible

By K. Connors

K. Connors

Table of Contents

Introduction

Most people are unwilling to face the truths of life. They are unable to confront their fears, so they end up as great dreamers but weak doers. They feel hopeless, limited and uninspired with few punches of life. Truth hurts, but by embracing them, you are giving yourself a clear head start to plan well. You don't get surprised when life throws you lemons. You can keep pushing through the worthy goals you set.

When you know what you'll face, you can incorporate wise actions to get the full benefit of life. You will reap the greatest return if you know how to respond.

Only a few people can welcome these truths. When you are open to the wisdom life gives, it will provide more valuable opportunities designed for you. It is a lot easier to be ignorant to the realities of life. However, the more time that we spend pretending that truths aren not a part of our reality, the more time that we waste not living in alignment with our true selves.

Is ignorance bliss? Absolutely not. The fact of the matter is that if we want to grow and expand, we need to be honest with ourselves.

We need to be willing to open our minds, and see the world through a different lens.

Below are 17 Controversial Truths We Choose to Ignore, Understand these brutal realities and anything is possible.

We Are Not Born Equal

We are not raised or treated equitably, it is up to you to compensate, not the world. Only you control your drive and ambitions. Your skin color, status, environment do not define you. The true definition of equality means that we all should have an equal opportunity to live up to our highest potential in regard to our desires and abilities.

That doesn't mean that we all will be equal in stature, financial standing, social standing, etc. It only means we should be given the equal opportunity to achieve the level of success we desire or are capable of achieving.

We are all born into different life situations with different life paths, for some, living a life of simplicity instead of becoming a social or political achiever is all they desire. For them to strive for a successful career in politics or business would be unnatural and against everything they were born to do.

Many think it is a government's job to make all things equal and to elevate those who haven not achieved the success others think they should have.

The best thing government can do is just get out of our way. We are more than capable of charting our own course and deciding how we want to live, solving our own problems and repaying our karma. We really do not need any help from anybody, instead we need to channel our energy to take charge of our life and make the most of it to be successful in whatever we decide to do.

Regretfully, in today's world, many have come to believe it is easier to let someone else run their life than it is for them to do so. It is easier to have someone else decide how much money they can make, to let the government provide health care, education and many other necessities of life.

Letting someone else run their life gives them more time to have fun and enjoy a beer after work, while giving responsibility to someone else. Then, when something does go wrong, they have someone to blame. They can then say it's not their fault and they didn't have anything to do with it. What they forget is that when others are providing all your wants and need, then they can take it all away in a heartbeat, which they can and will do at some point in time.

You have to take charge of your life. Many people have given away their power to their boss, spouse, family, environment, external influences, and friends. Whose life are you really living? Is it one of your own making? Or is it of another's making? Are you truly satisfied with the life that you are living? Look within, is this it from you? Is this all that you are capable of becoming and achieving?

If the answer is 'No,' you know deep down that you can become more and achieve more. There are no limits to what you can achieve; you can become the person you truly want to be and achieve all that you want to achieve.

Believe in yourself and take action. Never let anyone take control of your life, it is your life and you can live it in whatever way you choose to live it. Many have stumbled into a fake life, unaware that they have taken on someone else's life, they have become conditioned to be a slave in another's dream, rather than an architect of their own dreams.

Life can be joyous, magnificent, fulfilling, abundant, prosperous, and adventurous. However, many just choose to live the timid life, being led by others who have taken charge of their lives. Many have become so dependant on others to tell them when to wake up, when to go to sleep, what to eat, how to talk, how to work, and how to be as an individual. If you are not aware of who you are becoming you will end up being average.

The challenge is to take charge of your life, to design your life the way you want to live it, to do what you love to do, to spend your days pursuing things that interest you and bring a sense of joy and fulfillment. You do not have to spend your days doing things that you do not want to do, you can step out of the life of conformity by changing direction; set your sail on a new destination of success.

The answers that you seek are within you, there is no need to look outside of yourself, you know deep down within yourself who you want to be and how you want to live. If you could be anything and do anything that you wanted to do, what would that be? Start to ask yourself that question daily so that you start unplugging yourself from the system of mediocrity.

It is up to you if you want to make your dreams come true and for you to reach your full potential. You have got to step up your game, you have got to stop engaging in mediocrity, you have got to start engaging in 'Life Changing Tasks' on a daily basis that will move you from where you are to where you want to be. Visualize yourself being successful daily, and be in a state of appreciation for the life that you will be living soon.

It is so easy to let someone else dictate to you how to live your life, it is so easy to cower away and be resigned to a life of conformity and fearfulness, but you must take action in the direction of 'Your Dreams.' I am urging you to take charge of your life. Take charge of your life and design it the way you want it to be, otherwise, you will have to settle for the life that you don't want to live, and what a shame that will be. A few years from now what are you going to be doing in life? And who will you have become? Is what you are doing on a daily basis taking you to greater heights? Or is it confining you to a life of mediocrity?

Become aware that you can take charge of your life, you can make your dreams a reality, you can make a difference in the world, and you can live a life of greatness. Do not let life make you a coward like the masses, step into the arena of life and live your dreams.

K. Connors

If Emotions Control You, You Have Already Lost

Some of the most worst happenings human history has witnessed have been the result of emotions beyond control. People fall prey to negative emotions and make the wrong decisions or take adverse actions. Therefore, emotions are one of the most important part of human life; or rather human emotions apply to all areas of human life.

Can a person control their emotions? What can you really control? Happiness for everyone! We are obsessed with control these days. Every company, institution, agenda, and family member wants to have some sort of control over us, and we want it over them. We want our opinions to be heard and our needs to be met. We want the control. Why do we want this control? If we are in control, we are happy. Everyone feels this.

Once a person chooses to win the battle against their own emotions, then they have won the greatest victory of all. And, once a person wins that victory they have the power of influence in any situation. Don't all adults need this power of influence? When should this power be learned? Learning self-control should happen as soon as possible.

I believe that each person can effectively learn how to govern their own thoughts, behaviors, and emotions. Self-government is being able to determine the cause and effect of any given situation, and possessing a knowledge of your own behaviors so that you can control them

In order to asses your own behaviors and emotions and change them for the better it is essential to understand cause and effect. I am sure you have noticed grown adults who do not understand cause and effect well. These adults are the ones who yell to get their way, and ignore people to get their points across.

Being able to control our own thoughts, actions and emotions is a divine gift. It is called agency. We get to choose our own emotions in every situation. We cannot always choose every situation, but can always choose how we will respond to each situation we are in. This kind of control is the greatest gift we have. However, just as we have the control over our own lives and growth, we can also give it away. Control cannot be taken. It has to be given.

So how do you control emotions? Read on to find out.

Be Prepared

Sometimes, we feel a burst of emotion when we are caught unaware. When someone says something that we do not expect, we might cry, laugh or get really angry. This might be okay when you're among friends, but it is a different story altogether when you are in the middle of a board meeting.

One way on how to control emotions is to prepare yourself for what is ahead. For example, if you already know that you are meeting with an insufferable client, pace yourself. Tell yourself not to get hot-headed. Be the epitome of cool. Preparing yourself helps you control your emotions and not the other way around.

Be Objective

By separating yourself from the situation, you are able to look at things in a more logical perspective.

Let's say you are a journalist covering an earthquake tragedy where thousands of people died. If you want to learn how to control emotions long enough so you can do your job properly, detach yourself from the number of grieving people. Focus on the numbers and the science.

Learning how to control emotions might sound harsh and cold in a tragedy such as this; but sometimes, it is the only way you can do your job and report the incident properly.

Be Patient

Counting 1 to 10 will not help you if you are a pretty impatient person. Therefore, it is important that you work on that area of yourself. Being patient helps delay bursts of emotion that may not be appropriate for the situation. It gives your feelings time to subside and retreat.

One way to cultivate patience is meditation. This activity also helps you calm yourself down and quell strong waves of emotion.

Being able to feel emotions and express them is part of being human. There is nothing wrong with that. However, there are certain instances wherein we must learn how to control emotions. Besides, sudden bursts of emotions also lead us to doing things we might regret later on. In order to avoid any awkward situations, remember to be prepared, be objective and be patient.

Words Can Never Hurt You

People mostly tend to get angry or agitated due to the type of language or words used on them. You must have heard of the saying -- "Sticks and stones will break my bones but words would never hurt me." Use this saying whenever you are verbally abused by someone and you feel angry or agitated. Always learn to act smart and not angry.

K. Connors

Appearance Matters

It's a daily ritual — looking into the mirror and checking yourself whether you have got the right shoes on, clothed with a well-ironed shirt and those stunning jeans to wow people whenever you walk down through the busy streets. Yes. People, like you, love to look into the mirror and enjoy the beauty they see — your face, your body and everything that is you.

Looking good, not only in the mirror but in the eyes of people is very important. It cannot be considered a luxury for a person to want to look good, it is actually a natural human right. Yes, you are very much allowed to look good. And why not? Looking good is something that gives almost anyone a boost to live life much, much better, so looking your best can help a whole lot.

It Helps You Make A Great Impression

One of the top advantages of being presentable is that you can make a great first impression in front of other people. The last thing you want is to deal with any clothing issues -- all you have to do is to take your time and actively find the right way to dress professionally.

It is never easy to achieve all the results you have in mind, but if you pay attention to how you dress, you are bound to obtain some great results.

People Respect You More

Just put two people side by side, one that is dressed presentable and another person that is not groomed and see which has low quality, non-ironed clothes.

Of course, the presentable person will be more respectable, because they show how important it is to care about their image. So if you want people to respect you, then you must look presentable at all times.

You Can Explore a Variety of Styles

Being presentable is exciting since you can try out all kinds of different styles and ideas. You can feel free to experiment with being presentable and it will give you some extraordinary results every time.

You should always try to dress up smartly, with new and cool stuff being tried out all the time. It can make quite the difference, so you might as well give it a try for yourself and see how it works.

Higher Confidence Levels

You want to improve your confidence levels as much as you can. Being presentable helps you do that. It makes it easier for you to boost your trust in your own ideas. On top of that, you can reinforce the idea that you deserve the great results and success coming your way.

It Imbues a Sense of Responsibility

It's very important to be responsible and focused on your day to day life. Dressing sharply and being more presentable shows that you have that sense of responsibility and focus. People will take you more seriously, and that on its own can really make quite the difference all the time.

We encourage you to dress sharply as often as possible. Take grooming and personal hygiene very seriously too. And of course, always try to look as presentable as you can. Looks matter, and tha i's what you want to pursue the most.

Once you do that, nothing will stand in your way, and it will help make the experience a whole lot better. You can also experiment with the way you dress, sure, but make it as presentable and as professional as possible!

You Are Not What You Own, Don't Let It Define You

Whether its at work, at home, or in the community, most of us want to be successful, contributing members of society. Since some of our bars are set higher (or lower) than others, it is pretty obvious that what defines success will be different to each and every person. We all have different measures and definitions of what it means to be successful, and no one definition is right or wrong.

We are all familiar with these common success factors. Things like:

- Figuring out what you really love.
- Researching and working on your passion.
- Being responsible.
- Dreaming big.
- Working your butt off.

And while there are obviously several things missing from that list, one big idea in particular that is often overlooked is:

The number one thing you can do to ensure success personally and professionally is **add value.**

Let us take a look at what that even means...

Value itself is something that is defined by your customers, your people or your tribe, not you. This important point is often overlooked since we are usually so caught up in the work, the nitty-gritty details of our brilliant idea that we forget to come up for air and make sure we are still on course. It does not matter what you think is valuable; if the people you are trying to win over do not see the value in what you are doing, then there is none.

That said, each person is different and so the topic of value is highly subjective. So while what you have to offer may not be valued by everyone, there is likely a sub-group of people who are dying to know or see what you have to offer. How you are able to add value will differ from customer to customer. But the point is to remember that it is your customer that dictates what is valuable, not you.

Think of it this way: We have all been taught that the thought behind the gift is the most important thing. But if your focus when giving a gift is really on the recipient and not on yourself, then you want to give them something they want and can use/appreciate/admire.

So How Can You Add Value in Other Areas of Life?

There are several ways you can add value on a daily basis, and the things you do or offer need not be huge or earth shattering. Many truly valuable things aren't.

1. Talk to People

It's that simple. Find out who your people are and ask them what they want. Yes, ask them. Talk to them at the grocery store, on the playground, in the boardroom or send out a survey. Ask them about their fears, their desires, or what that one thing is that would make their lives easier. Building a product, creating a report or finishing a chore might make you feel great, but if it is never used or valued, is it really worth it? Could your efforts be better focused elsewhere?

2. Check In

While you go through your day, check what you are doing against these ideas of how you can be adding value:

- Do something incredibly useful.
- Solve a problem that has yet to be solved.
- Be accessible, approachable and helpful.

- Teach a new skill.

- Allow people to escape and forget their problems.

There are a number of things we can do to add value on a daily basis. But to be effective at it, we need to get out of our own heads, step away from our own agendas and see what we can bring to the table. You do not have to create something new to stand out; just do it better and offer more than what is already available.

If You Are Not Enjoying Your Life, You Are Just Dying

Life is short, this is a known fact even if you are able to live to the age of 100+ you are never going to live more than that. So for that reason you really need to make sure that the life that you lead is one that is full of enjoyment. For life is short, and what is the purpose of living if you are not able to enjoy the few short years you may have on this planet.

We all want to live a happy life and the secret is to enjoy life without having to make excuses that you don't have enough time or money. You can start enjoying your life now with what you already have. Add excitement to your life and that does not always mean that you need to go on a vacation. You can still have fun while doing your daily routine or use your personal time to do exciting things.

There are many things that people can do to enjoy life, but it is a shame when you look around and you see that people often waste their lives in the accumulation of things that do not matter. Being an avid consumer will not give you any pleasure in the long term. The only thing that will do, is make you realize that you have wasted your short life just consuming and not living. Life again is quite short and it should not be wasted on such frivolous activities.

So, how are you supposed to go about enjoying the life you have worked so hard to build for yourself? Try relaxing for a few moments and enjoying it with what you have.

1. Surround Yourself with People That Makes You Happy (Positive People)

The first and most important thing that you can do to enjoy life more is to make sure that every day you are doing things and you are surrounding yourself with people that make you happy. Step away and avoid those situations and people that make you sad. You really do not want to involve yourself with people that are going to cause you to be sad, instead you need to maximise your time with the people that you love and that will give you joy.

2. Cut Out the Activities That Bring Less Joy to You

The next thing that you can do to really enjoy life is to cut out the activities that are not bringing you any joy, but are just causing you to waste your time on this precious planet. Really, there is no time for doing these things which you do not like. Instead you need to be maximising your time with activities that you love doing and love surrounding yourself with.

3. Take Life Slowly

You really need to be able to slow down and enjoy every single moment of it. You need to understand that your life is a lot more interesting and enjoyable when you are able to slow things down, so that you are really living in the moment. So try really hard to focus your time and your energies toward making life more enjoyable.

We all have been given one life to live. Live every moment of life because you do not know what is going to happen in the very next moment. Make the most of every opportunity that crosses your path. Reach out for newer, richer, deeper, life-changing experiences. And use those experiences as a means for personal growth and pushing the boundaries of yourself mentally, spirituality, and intellectually for the betterment of yourself and the world at large.

K. Connors

Thinking and Doing Are Not the Same Thing

To "do" means to take action. To implement the things you have been putting off doing. Thinking is passive. It is comfortable because it does not require very much out of us. Doing is active. We avoid doing because it requires a lot of time and energy. Frankly, most of us just don't have enough of that at the end of the day.

Critique and discard the lies you tell yourself. Force your promising thoughts into plans. Force those into productive actions. Be optimistic only about what your own persistence and actions will do for your life and mission.

Following these tips will help you to stop putting your energy toward thinking, and focus it on doing instead.

If you have been involved in in a business for any length of time, you know that there are a million different reports and a million different people telling you what to do. They are probably giving you excellent advice.

The trouble is, it takes so much out of you to actually to follow through with your plans and "do". You know what it takes to be successful. The next level is to actually take those steps and achieve your goals.

What you need is a solid plan. You need some actions that will stop your brain from thinking, and catapult you into action.

Some of these tips will help you immediately; others will take a lot longer to sink in. Still others may not mean much to you now, and will come into practice at a later time in your life. Let these tips work their magic on you, and start seeing success immediately.

Of course, your procrastination won't be cured by osmosis. You are going to have to apply them to the fullest extent possible. You alone hold the keys to your success, but these tips can guide you there.

Admit That You Have A Problem

This sounds like a line from a recovery program. Yet, it can work wonders in helping you to overcome your procrastination problem. Admit that you are a procrastinator, and the other tips will sink in beautifully.

It is easy enough to blame others for our problems. You can say "oh, the baby was fussy so I didn't get any work done" or "they didn't give that to me in time so I couldn't do it." However, these are excuses. Admit that you alone hold the keys to your success, and you will go a long way toward overcoming procrastination.

K. Connors

Say "I Don't Want to Procastinate Anymore!"

Saying things out loud gives them power. You need this power in order to take control of the problem. You DO NOT want to procrastinate anymore, so make it so. Actions speak louder than words, but these words can help guide you.

Admit Guilt If You Have Some

Some people may always feel very guilty when they procrastinate. You may have a constant nagging feeling that you should be doing the work you have been putting off for ages.

If you have this guilt, admit it. Admission will help get a load off of your mind. You will be surprised at how light you will feel once you pinpoint the guilt and own it.

Some people may not feel guilty. If that is the case for you, you may have bought the eBook because there was a feeling you should fix your procrastination problem, but you didn't feel much guilt. That is okay!

Take Stock of Your Procrastination, grab a pen and paper. Now, … not later!

Ask yourself what things you are currently procrastinating on. Write these down!

It may seem silly to write them down since your responsibilities are constantly swarming in your head. However, getting details down on paper gives your mind space to breath. Your mind can only hold so much in without feeling overwhelmed. Then, guess what happens? You get the urge to procrastinate because you cannot deal with it all.

So, get it all down on paper. This will help you to stop thinking, and start doing.

If you're having trouble getting started, here are some ideas to jog your memory. You may have trouble:

- Paying bills on time
- Returning phone calls
- Answering emails
- Folding laundry

You get the idea. There are any number of things we procrastinate with on a daily basis.

34

Use these methods to motivate yourself whenever you feel like procrastinating; make them a mantra and repeat them in your mind whenever you are feeling lazy or overwhelmed. Over a period of time you will realize that you have become a do-er and a go-getter.

K. Connors

Money, Fame, and Success Can Make You Happy

Few things are prized more in our western cultures than money, fame and success. The message is strong and clear: you get money, you get happiness. The more money, the more happiness. It is laced into all of our commercials, it is laced into the very fiber of our society. Money and fame buys happiness.

Of course you and I are not so foolish as to buy into this get happy quick scheme. After all we have endless examples of people with incredible wealth and very little happiness.

And yet, still, some little part of you holds out. The illusion has been planted deep within. Money is fun. A lot of money would be the thing that would tip the scales forever in your favor for major happiness.

No, money does not buy happiness per se, but it sure would make things so much easier. Or would it? Financial freedom would give you peace of mind which means once you can spend your money in the right way, it can give you happiness and below are ways you can do that.

Eliminating Financial Anxiety

The reason that money demonstratively increases happiness levels up until the point where it takes a certain salary to feel financially secure.

Having enough money means no anxiety when shopping at the grocery store, going out to eat or paying your rent. This type of security is overlooked when you are used to it.

Remembering and being appreciative of the fact that you are free to purchase things, though, will make you happier even after it has settled in as normal amount of your finances. Fundamentally, having enough money to buy these basic necessities will no doubt increase your happiness levels.

Buy Experiences

Money can lend you the opportunity to have memorable experiences. Although you do not need a lot of money to have certain experiences, to travel the world and do so comfortably, significant amounts of money can go a long way. Therefore, spending money on experiences will give you many moments of happiness as well as positive memories to look back on.

One important point to note is that the experiences you pay for should be ones that you genuinely enjoy, not just things that society values. If you hate going to concerts, for example, then splurging to go to a show is not a good use of your money.

This is despite how many others might tell you they are jealous. Instead, you should buy experiences you truly enjoy. The examples are endless but include vacations, sporting events, nice meals, tours and shows.

Money can also enable you to learn new things. You could buy musical instrument lessons or pay for a fitness instructor to get into better shape. Picking up new skills and finding hobbies that we love will make us happier. Consequently, it is worthwhile to spend money to get more out of your hobbies and interests.

Give to Charity

Giving back to others also makes us happier. Sharing your wealth with those who need it can go a long way in others' lives. Being able to see the impact you are making is a warm feeling. Subsequently, wealth gives you a larger opportunity to give to charity and leave an impact that will leave both others and yourself better off.

Help Loved Ones

Another great way to spend money is on people you care about. Helping a sibling, parent or friend through a tough time can be a great feeling. Even being able to throw extra money into a birthday party for your child or a good friend will make you happier.

Without higher levels of wealth, it can be difficult to rationalize putting money into things like this. When you have the opportunity, though, it will make you happier.

Buy Things That Give You Free Time

An underrated way to spend your money is on saving yourself time. There are many tasks we do throughout the day that we do not enjoy. These differ for everyone, but examples might include doing the laundry, cooking, and driving and doing household chores.

When you have more money, you can spend it on eliminating these meaningless tasks. You can pay others to do them for you or find ways to automate them with technology. Doing so will free up time so you can do more of what you love.

Some Items Are Also Valuable

One of the largest struggles faced with buying things is that, although they are novel and exciting at first, they become normalized and you forget to appreciate them. That is why, generally, experiences tend to create higher happiness levels than items.

Of course, this is not always the case. Buying things you will be able to frequently appreciate and use often will generally make you happier.

One good example is art. If you are someone who enjoys art, then buying paintings and pictures for your house will make you happier. You will frequently see them and can take the time whenever you would like to appreciate and admire them. Find what is important to you, then make time on your schedule for it.

K. Connors

Life Is a Competition

Everyone wants to ensure that they become the best at whichever endeavor, sport, or activity they are engaged in. It does not matter if it is in academics, sports or one's career. If you are engaged in a venture you are passionate about, you will desire to be the best at it.

Life is a competition, but it is not a race against anyone else. Rather, the real journey is only against yourself and unrealized potential.

It is easy to compare yourself against other people especially as they flood our screens with images. But when you compete against other people, you judge yourself based on their values and metrics. The problem with this is even if you win, you only do something that is important to them, not you.

The most important part of competing against yourself is the ability to set your own values and metrics. You choose the goals that fit you best, and what you really want to compete on - and what you don't.

And, yeah, sometimes you lose. You might do worse than you did before. Some days, it is just enough not to take a step backward. And others, when you least expect it, you bound forward.

Either way, when you compete with yourself, you will not be lured into other people's competition and their values. Move forward but only evaluate yourself based on meaningful things. Smile, nod, and then forget it when other people try to entice you into competing. Only you can decide what really matters to you.

If you find yourself comparing yourself with your friend, co-worker, neighbor, or partner, you need to stop this minute. Comparing yourself with others is the easiest way to lose focus and distract yourself from your goals. As a human being, the best favor you can do yourself and the world at large is to be laser focused on your personal goals and on your definition of what success with those goals mean to you.

1. Write down Your Goals

Writing down your goals is one of the easiest ways to keep in touch with your inner purpose and see where you would like to be in a given time frame. Research has shown time and time again that writing down your goals dramatically increases your chances of achieving them. When writing your goals, it is important to write down the steps you have taken or plan to take to accomplish them. Also, make sure your goals are Specific, Measurable, Active, Realistic, and Timed (S.M.A.R.T) to increase your chance of success.

2. Track Your Progress

Next, track your progress. This would give you a sense about how far you are in your journey towards improving your art. Getting a good sense of your progress, helps you determine areas in which you need to improve or work harder. It also reassures you that you are on track if you are meeting all your set targets for yourself.

3. Devise a Plan for Improvement

Now that you have reviewed your goals, devise a plan for improvement that can help you perfect it. Since you have the best understanding of what the best expression of your art should look like, come up with action steps that can help you improve to the best of your ability and that can help you reach your definition of success.

However, if you follow these three steps, you will find yourself more productive and also be in a healthy competition with yourself.

Everyone Is Wearing Different Masks Depending on The Occasion.

Being a conscientious person is being someone others can count on. Have you ever worked, studied, or played a sport with someone who you could not rely on? The person who seems to constantly let you down.

Examples like:

- The colleague who missed the project deadline she promised she would meet.

- The classmate who skipped town the same weekend a team assignment is due.

- The sports teammate who consistently missed practice.

I cannot tell if they truly did not remember their commitment, think no one will notice, or expect someone else will pick up after them.

Why Is Conscientiousness Important?

How you follow through on an agreement either makes people trust you or distrust you. If you agreed to reach a place at 3:45 pm and walked in at 3:46 pm, you are late and there is probability of people losing trust in you immediately. You have to constantly remind yourself of all commitments.

What is Conscientiousness?

Conscientiousness is a personality trait describing someone who is cautious, diligent, and does the right thing. A person with this trait understands how their actions affect others. Those who rank high on the conscientious scale are more empathetic toward others, live longer, and are more successful.

What Does Conscientiousness Predict?

Conscientiousness is one of the big five traits considered valuable for leaders. I dare say it is a critical success factor for any goal you want to pursue. Even if you are creative, or a visionary, responsibility is the stuff that helps you realize your vision.

If you are part of a team of individuals who are conscientious and dependable, then you are organized and goal-oriented. A study of selling performance found that conscientious sales persons outperformed their non-conscientious peers.

How Can You Improve Your Conscientiousness?

1. Do what you said you would do

The primary way to gain trust is to consistently do what you said you were going to do. When you say you will send out the report by 5:00 or you'll call, do it.

2. Show up on time

Equally important to doing what you said you were going to do is doing it on time. Showing up on time contributes to being seen as a conscientious person.

Whether it's a meeting, practice or class, try to not be even one minute late. It is noticeable.

As a reminder, repeat to yourself: No one cares that you are busy because everyone else is busy too.

Record commitments in a calendar

Use technology to mitigate bad memory. If you are the "I forget almost everything a few minutes after hearing about it" person, you can become a serial note taker. Set a personal goal to avoid missing deadlines.

- Estimate how much time a task would take and create it in the calendar.

- Add a task to the calendar at least three days before its due.

Setting the task for a few days ahead is like setting your alarm to go off 15 minutes before you actually have to get up. This method buys extra time and is helpful when unexpected stuff shows up. Successful people do not typically say, "I'm busy." Harvard researchers advise that saying you are too busy to meet a commitment will label you as a self-important person and hurt your career.

Communicate Early If You Will Be Late

Most people appreciate being told as early as possible. Always try to avoid taking this step as much as possible because it breaks the first rule of being conscientious. Understand that trust can be lost quickly and can take longer to rebuild. It is because of the risk of trust loss that it is neccesary to do everything possible to prevent lateness.

K. Connors

Learn to Adapt or Stay Poor

Have you ever taken the wrong road or just found yourself on a dark, eerie street where you are trying to look calm, but inside your gut instincts are screaming, "Get me out of here and fast because I'm scared, lost, and this does not feel right!"?

Maybe in this very moment, you find that your life may have led you to a dark alley, a wrong turn, or you know you have temporarily strayed from the right path.

Your instincts tell you they want a new, better life; one where you are not settling or struggling. Then the overwhelming task appears in front of you, like a needle in a hay stack, that you must change the path of your destiny. Where do you begin and how do you even know what the first step is in proceeding forward?

Follow these seven steps to change your life taking you from overwhelmed to clarity, confidence, and action.

1. What needs to change?

Ask yourself what needs to happen or what do you need to change that would improve your life or steer it in a new direction? When you clearly define what you need to change, it places your target front and center giving you a focus to propel action towards.

2. Explore and Brainstorm All Opportunities and Possibilities

Take some time and seek support from others to brainstorm and discover all the opportunities and possibilities for what this change could be. Outline in detail what each possible scenario would look like, what it would give you or bring to your life, and how it could be created. When you brainstorm, it is important to always include possibilities that seem grand or outside the norm of what you might normally think of. Let yourself dream, stretch your thinking beyond its regular boundaries, and ask for assistance from others who are different from you and who will offer alternative options.

3. How do you need to change and how does your life need to change?

The reason you need to ask yourself, "How might I need to change?", is that it may be you are standing in your own way on one small element. Sometimes when you take a moment to look at where you find yourself and then look at how you may have contributed to this in any way, there may be one small factor that if recognized, could positively transform your life. It could be recognizing that you are paralyzed by rejection, or you hold a belief that limits your potential, or a part of your personality that if brought to your consciousness and monitored, would allow you to break free from stagnation. Maybe, the spotlight of attention needs to be directed more on how your life needs to change in order to open yourself up to a new path.

- What do you need to let go of?
- Who do you need to become?
- Do you need to rearrange, prioritize or expand your life for this change?

4. Grow, Learn, Adapt

To really change and transform your life, one must be willing to grow, learn, and adapt.

- In which way(s) do you need to grow in order to make this new journey successful?
- What lesson did you need to learn, or have you learned, that will positively take you where you want to go?
- What new skills or knowledge do you need to acquire for this next adventure?
- Is there anywhere you need to adapt to be more flexible?

5. Identify the Unmet Needs Behind the Desire to Change

When we need to make a change in our lives, it is usually because a personal need is not being met. That need may be financial, emotional, physical, spiritual or something else personal for you.

- What are the needs that you want this change to address?
- What are the values that support this change?
- How will it feel and what does it look like to fulfill these needs?

6. Desire, Motivation, & Vision for Change

Your desire, motivation, and vision are the fuel to fire your change. When you take the time to define, detail, and clarify these, they will keep the momentum of your goal moving forward at a steady pace.

- Write out and define your desire, motivation, and vision for this change
- What is important to you about this change?
- How will it improve your life?
- What will it give you and what does it look like?

7. Make a Decision, Create a Plan, Take the First Step

Decide on the change you will make and what the first step on your new path will be. This is a crucial step as many of us may get stuck in fear and indecision thereby keeping us stationary and motionless. The good news is that you can take a few steps in one direction to explore and if it does not feel right, you can change direction.

The key is to begin, to experiment, explore, be curious, courageous, and adventurous. Adjust your sails if need be, but set sail for your destination and always learn to adapt to situations. However, never stay long in an uncomfortable one.

K. Connors

Happiness Comes from What You Can Do For Others

Happiness is a state of mind. It is not measured by the number of material possessions that you have, or by how much money is in the bank. You can have all the things in life that you need and want, but that does not necessarily make you happy.

There are many people in large families with very little money, but they are happy with their lives. It cannot therefore be money or material possessions that bring happiness.

I believe that it is the small acts of kindness and caring that you show to others that really makes the difference to your happiness levels.

There are some simple things you can do every day with and for the ones around you to help them to be happier. They do not necessarily cost anything and can change their lives.

Inspire and Motivate

You know how good it feels when someone inspires and motivates you to be all that you can be in your life. This is one of the easiest things you can do for someone to help them find happiness in their life. Find ways to inspire and motivate people. Sometimes all it takes is a pat on the back and telling them that you believe in them.

Make Them Laugh

One of the easiest and most enjoyable ways of helping others feel happy is to make them laugh. You know this one will work. Haven't you ever been feeling down, had someone come along that made you laugh and then you were all of a sudden in a better mood? Laughter really does help to make people happy. So learn what makes those around you laugh and make sure you make someone else laugh at least once a day. It will make them, and yourself, happier.

Give a Hug

One of the best things for a persons level of happiness is physical touch. We all need physical touch on a regular basis, but in our individualistic modern society we often do not touch enough, and we definitely do not hug enough. So go out and give someone a hug. It can work wonders. If you don't believe me go to YouTube and look for "free hugs" and see just how happy the people are after they get the free hug from a stranger. It can work wonders.

An Unexpected Gift at an Unexpected Time

This is a great life lesson learned from the movie "Finding Forrester". In this movie, the lead tells the young man the way to win a girl's heart is an unexpected gift at an unexpected time. This is a wonderful lesson and one that works for making anyone happy, not just the person you are pursuing romantically. Who doesn't love to get gifts? Unfortunately we are conditioned to only get them on certain occasions like birthdays or Christmas (or whatever holiday you celebrate) or anniversaries, etc. How much happier would someone be if they got an amazing gift for no reason other than you wanted them to have a gift. Give it a try, who knows, maybe you will get one in return.

Tell Them You Love Them

This is the final and simplest way of making someone happier. Just tell them that you love them. The key here is you have to mean it.

This will make a person's day, and it will make you happier as well. Love is a powerful thing and sadly we just do not say it and share it enough. People need to hear that they are loved. I have yet to find someone who was not in a better mood after hearing "I Love You".

Be a Living Example of How It Is Don

The best way to help someone find happiness is to live a life full of happiness yourself. By doing so you will automatically show people that it is possible to live a life full of happiness. Not only that but you will be a living inspiration to countless people. Plus, since you know how to do it, you will have a much easier time teaching others how to succeed in living a happy life as well.

So open up and give to other people every day. Use one of these simple techniques to make their day a little bit better. Everyone wants more happiness in their life and now you know how to give it to them. So do not be selfish, get out there and give happiness. It is free and can change the world.

Being Busy Does Not Mean What You Are Doing Is Worthwhile

Busy is one of the most overused words. We hear all the time, "I'm too busy," or "I don't have time." How often do you actually achieve results while you are busy? Not too often, I bet. Switch your focus from being busy to being productive, so that you can accomplish more, see tangible results, and have time for fun.

There is a big difference between being busy and being productive. Do you know the difference? Which one fills most of your time? We all have the same 24 hours in a day, but how you spend those 24 hours will determine if you are really being intentional with your time.

Most times, we spend a lot of time on things that are not productive or important while forgetting that self development, health, relationships, self-maintenance, freedom, security, is what is important.

Below are some of the things you can do to keep yourself productive doing things that are important.

Establish a Workflow

By creating systems and processes for your daily tasks, you will be able to spend less time figuring out what to do next and more time actually doing it. Use the same workflow for similar tasks in order to create a checklist for yourself on what needs to be done. For example, you can create a workflow for your client work, blog posts, social media, newsletter, or design process.

In addition, creating editorial calendars and scheduling your social media and blog posts can be a big time saver. This also goes back to batching your tasks. For example, if you create an editorial calendar in advance, you have your blog topics ready to go and can spend less time deciding what to write about. Then you can write the posts, follow your workflow, and schedule it to publish when needed.

Remove Distraction

What distractions around you decrease your productivity? Visual distractions include piles of papers or unfinished projects, and even sticky notes on your computer. Auditory distractions are generally sounds that pull your focus from your project.

Turn off dings, alarms, notification alerts, popups and sounds that you can control. Distractions and interruptions can fool us into thinking we are being productive, while destroying your focus.

Make Three Or Four Clear Priorities For Yourself Each Day

If you have too many priorities, you will be really busy, but probably not that successful. In order to be productive we have to prioritize, make time for, and concentrate on the most important things in life to us. Saying, "yes," to every opportunity that comes our way is a recipe for not being very productive. So before saying "yes," make sure it fits your priorities.

Say "No"

There is only so much time in a day. You do not have time to do everything. Saying "yes" to too many commitments is probably the easiest and most annoying way to pack your calendar way too full.

You do not have to do everything everyone asks you to do. You can say "no" without feeling bad about it.

Once you cultivate most of the points, you will start being productive with your activities and stop being busy with things that are not worthwhile.

Everyone Dies, Even You

Remember one day you will be dead, but don't be afraid of death, embrace it, use it as a strength to live life to the fullest

A fulfilled life is when you live large and experiment with everything before you die — actually, this is the greatest hoax of human existence. Think about death often and see how fulfilled your life routine turns out to be.

Death is inevitable and thinking about it should be too. Death is possibly the only inevitable event in life. Everyone and everything that lives will eventually die.

But what if we embraced death, talked about it more and shared our own vulnerable thoughts, feelings and questions about it? While for some of us this may seem uncomfortable, undesirable or even a little weird, think how liberating it would be if we are willing to face the reality of death directly.

Death is always there, standing patiently by our side, accompanying us in every step we take, and at any moment we might suddenly lose ourselves in its embrace. And one thing is certain: We are all going to die.

Life's journey might be quite unpredictable, but that part of it called death is not. Sure, we might not be able to tell when exactly we are going to die, but we know without doubt that we will. In other words, death is inevitable, and as the saying goes, the very moment we were born we were sentenced to die.

Yet most of us do not like to think about death, and even pretend that it will not happen to us any time soon. For years upon years we constantly hear about others dying around us, yet we blindly believe that we will not be the next one to die.

We do not pay much attention to the power death has upon us, not because we do not care about it — on the contrary, we care so much that the very idea of death scares the hell out of us. Or, to put it differently, death scares us to death! No wonder we are doing anything we can to avoid thinking about it.

Recall the last time you had an in-depth conversation with someone about death. It probably was not recently, right? Then ask yourself how many times you have had such a conversation in your life. I bet they were not that many, or am I wrong?

Death is a taboo subject in our culture, something we should not openly discuss. But why exactly is that? Why does death frighten us so much that we do not even find it appropriate to talk about it?

The answer is attachment. We are so attached to the kind of life we are used to living that we cling to it as much as we can, to make sure it will not flee from us. W are attached to our partners, our possessions, and many other things we would be devastated to lose. We want them to belong to us, and we do our best to keep them in our lives.

Yet, all of our efforts are in vain. Life is ever-changing, continually moving, flowing, and no matter how hard we try to control it, it always disappoints us by escaping our tight fist of clinging and taking its own unpredictable course. And eventually death will unapologetically take all that we have away from us, leaving us with empty hands, not having anything left to hold on to.

Ultimately, all relationships are short-term relationships — they end quickly, even if they last for a lifetime (considering the infinite vastness of time). And just like death will take our partners away from us, it will also take away our material possessions. In fact, they were never ours — we only borrowed them from existence, and that is just for a little while. So let us savor what we've got while we can and make the most of out of our lives, by immersing ourselves in the present moment and squeezing all the good juice out of it.

This is why you need to embrace death because sooner or later, it will catch up with us all and it should be embraced like an old friend, one you cannot wait to tell all the amazing things you have gone through, all the achievements you have under your belt, all the stories about your children and your own life, and how in this tiny spec of time, you were a part of it. There is beauty in the finality of things and it makes everything we do so important. Best to LIVE, instead of just exist.

Small Problems Now Won't Matter in Five Years to Come

In life, high school and college have been filled with decision making. Some of the decisions are small and will probably end up being pretty irrelevant, and others could really impact your life. Most times people suffer so much stress and anxiety, sometimes completely unnecessary amounts, because of certain decisions people tend to overthink.

Meanwhile, because of all the stress and anxiety from worrying too much, you tend to start feeling unhealthy. A majority of people experience this feeling.

Let's say you sre in a situation where you have to make a decision and it seems like a huge one. You spend a lot of time thinking about it, trying to figure out what to do. You start to feel yourself stressing out, wondering how you will make it out of this moment alive. Well, here is a new rule to live by. In that moment, ask yourself, "Is this decision I am about to make going to matter to me in five years?" More than half the time, the chances are no, it will not. So, if it will not matter to you in five years, please don't let it bother you for more than five minutes.

Here is an example. Let us say your friends are pressuring you into something. Maybe to go out, maybe to do something big or small you do not want to, or hang with a certain group you do not care for much. But you start to feel like if you do not do what they are asking you, it is going to really upset them and make them mad at you for the night. Of course, you do not want to deal with that, so you suck it up and do the thing that does not cause you any pleasure or happiness. This is where the five year rule comes into place. Ask yourself, "Is this specific situation and the outcome of it going to matter to me in five years?" If not, say no to the situation and do what makes you happy. Because I promise you, in five years, what is going to matter is the memories you made doing what made you happy at the time. In five years, what is going to matter is all the A's you got in your classes because you chose to stay in and study instead of going out each weeknight. In five years, what you chose to do will matter more than what you forced yourself to do or how you forced yourself to feel. It is really the truth.

Below are the five steps that are very direct and simple to follow. If you follow these five steps on a daily basis, you will see the amount of good that continues to manifest in your life. As you begin to take action on these steps you will see really good results in your life.

Step 1

Get clear on the agenda. Make sure that you put your attention on the goal and block all else. Work with a solid team of intelligent people that can help you make clear decisions and move the project forward. The more clear and specific you and your teammates get on your agenda the better the results at the end.

Step 2

Will this matter in five years? A lot of times we get in situations where we begin to question why we got involved in the project to begin with. But if you get stuck in this situation, ask yourself if this will matter in five years time. If the answer is yes, continue forward. Realize the value of what you are doing and honor it. This bigger thinking perception will allow you to see the world in a very different way. Begin now to see the big picture, and use your intuition to guide you.

Step 3

If it is something you are passionate about and you stick to the agenda with clear purpose and appropriate actions, it will be completed with success. This is because you have put in the factors that matter: clarity, purpose, and action.

Step 4

One of the best ways to stay focused is to consistently review your goals. Make a point to schedule regular check-ins for yourself each week to check up on your progress. Ask yourself whether you kept on track towards your goals or if you were sidetracked during the week. What items can you seek to correct for the following week?

Step 5

It is hard to know what to focus on if you sre constantly in motion, running from one thing to another. Try taking some down time just for yourself. Read a good book, watch the tide come in at the beach, go for a walk in the park, or just sit quietly at home. Spending some time alone can help put things in perspective.

K. Connors

You Are a Tiny Organism on a Small Rock Floating Through Space

We can be significant to ourselves and to those around us.

From the time we were young, we may have been taught that we are not enough as we are. People would not accept us the way we are. They wanted us to think, look and behave in different ways. It is a fundamental human desire for connection and social relationships because we are, at our core, relational beings. Many of us chose to compromise, and are afraid that we would otherwise be left alone, isolated and helpless.

So we had to find ways to convince those around us that we are worth their friendship and act in certain ways to please others. In other words, we had to pretend. We may have learned to cover ourselves well with the veil of pretence. As adults, we may have a dozen masks to hide behind. So, Behind every mask lies a deep-rooted fear: the fear to express yourself and reveal to others who you truly are. When we blend in and try to be what we think others want, our life does not feel very satisfactory because, well, it is not our life. It is based on a false version of us.

Do we really have to ask ourselves whether we are happy? The truth is, something inside of us already knows the answer if we have to ask the question in the first place. When we are genuinely happy, we know. When we are not, we know that, too. Exposing our true selves, fully embracing our deepest desires, and facing our fears requires a tremendous amount of courage. Many of us have been trying to please others for such a long time, that we may have forgotten who we are and what is truly important to us. We have forgotten how to express ourselves, to be spontaneous and to recognize what we truly enjoy doing.

Imagine putting all of the energy we use in pretending into cultivating ourselves and creating something better of our being. Imagine dropping our pretence to build honest and healthy relationships? Only by then do I believe we can be significant to ourselves in particular and to those around us.

Be Honest with Yourself and Those You Come In Contact

When we lie, we put ourselves in constant anxiety because each lie must be covered up by another lie, and it goes thus. Being honest is the best way to be at peace with you and with others.

Do What You Love

No matter what others expect from you, try not to compromise your way of life. Whatever you enjoy doing, keep on doing it.

Be Rea

The only way to really connect with others on a meaningful level is to let them see who we are and to share our experience and what makes us tick. Not everyone will like it and that is okay. It really is. We increase our self worth not by being what others want us to be, but by being true to ourselves. If this feels like a struggle at the moment, you may consider talking to a therapist who can help in building confidence and in rediscovering who you really are; despite what others may think, there is zero shame in speaking with a licensed therapist.

Control Your Emotions

A part of respecting yourself is learning how to handle your emotions without causing more problems for your self. When we let our rage and hurt out in a damaging way, it only causes us to embarrass ourselves, destroy relationships, and leads to low self-respect which affects our relationships with people around us. There is a saying that the way you present yourself is the way people accept you.

Increase Your Knowledge

Develop interests and passions. Find a hobby. Learn as much as you can. Learning about things going on in the world around you will expand your brainpower and understanding, and will let you speak intelligently to a wide variety of people you meet. As you explore all the different opportunities this world has to offer, you will learn more about what you personally have to offer back to the people around you. There are so many people who live in such a small world, they feel others would never value their opinions and what they know. They see themselves as stupid or dumb. The way you see yourself is the way you will act. It happens every time.

You Always Have A Choice

We are making choices with every breath we take. We choose when we get up, when we go to sleep, when we eat, what we eat, when we check our email, when we play, when we exercise, when we rest, when we clean, when we work, what we wear, what we drive, where we shop, and the list goes on and on.

We choose how and with whom we communicate, how we respond to others' communication, what we believe, what we perceive, how we think, how we express ourselves, and what we do to survive. We choose our lovers and our friends, our enemies and our allies. We choose our sorrow, our joy, our inspiration and our discouragement. Yes, we make choices every moment of our lives, although many will argue relentlessly to the contrary.

Have you ever felt like you were backed against a wall or like you just did not have a choice in a particular situation? You are not alone for feeling this way. However, it is important to note that you always have a choice. Sometimes people feel like they have no choice and like they have to take the one path that seems most obvious and seems to be the only path. However, this thinking is wrong.

You always have a choice in the matter and you do not have to continue to be a victim of circumstance. Even if it seems like things are not always happening easily for you, there are still choices to be made in the matter. You do not have to sit idly by and let things happen to you. The kind of life you have is the kind of life that you choose for yourself.

You do not have anyone else to blame but yourself for how your life turns out. You can choose to have a happy life or you can choose to have a miserable life. Once you learn that the power lies in your hands, you become empowered. Empowered to do something about the life that you are living.

If you are not happy with the path that you are on, it is in your control to do something about it. You can choose to live a hectic and busy life or you can choose a calm and relaxed life. You can choose to live a healthy life and take care of your body and mind.

In order to take control of your life and choose the path that you want, you need to be disciplined. This means that you need to exert the effort that it takes to achieve your goals. You need to have goals and then also a plan to reach those goals.

If there are areas of your life that need improving, it is up to you and nobody else, to recognize these areas and complete a plan to make these improvements. Do you want to earn more money? The power to do so is in your hands.

Do you want to have more free time, lose weight, be healthier, spend more time with your kids or your spouse? If you want to achieve these goals, it is time to stop allowing excuses to get in your way. Do not blame other people or circumstance for your failures or short-comings. Take the initiative and reach your goals starting today. When it comes to improving your life, you always have a choice. No one can take that away from you.

K. Connors

Don't Complain About Things Out of Your Control

As human beings we worry a lot, sometimes about things we cannot control. That is why we decided to go through a list of things that are beyond your grasp, which you have no direct strings to pull in order to alter the outcome.

Life can be full of difficulties and sometimes our fears can overtake our sense of reason. However, if you allow your anxieties about things you cannot control to consume you, you will find it hard to live a life that is joyful and happy. Stop worrying about things you cannot control by managing and diminishing your worries through practicing self care and finding ways to limit your fears. You can also work to challenge any negative thoughts that you may have by considering the facts and finding reasonable alternatives to your anxiety.

Some things in life you cannot control. Why even try and get more disappointed right? The cards you have been dealt are for you to use to the best of your abilities, and if you need to bluff at times to succeed, then go for it. It is important to work towards your common goal and do everything you can to reach your destination. Below are some practical examples of how you can let go of things you cannot control.

1. Accept the things you cannot change

One of the reasons we worry too much is because we tend to focus on problems that are beyond our ability to solve, or things we cannot control. For example, we are planning a birthday celebration during the weekend and we worry about whether it will rain or not. Of course, there is a possibility for it to rain. So, instead of worrying about it, why not be flexible and have an alternative plan? This will ease your worries.

2. Do not try to guess what is on someone's mind

Sometimes we try to create our own story about what is going on in a person's mind even if in actuality, we do not have any idea. For example, if we said something a little bit off to a friend or a colleague which is not intentional, we automatically assume that they are mad at us. We then paint a picture of their enraged faces so that we lose hours of sleep because of worry. However, our fears are often just our imagination.

Trying to assume what is on someone's mind is most of the time useless and a waste of energy. Our mind is capable of creating scenarios that are both exaggerated and sometimes, even dangerous.

3. Spend more time in the present moment

There is nothing wrong with reminiscing about the past from time to time especially if you are thinking about something that inspires you. However, spending too much time in the past can pose some problems.

"When you spend too much time reliving the past in your mind then it is easy to start feeding your worries about the future. When you spend too much time in the future then it is also easy to get swept away by disastrous scenarios."

The wisest thing you can do is just focus your time and attention in the present where you have the power to decide what works for you and carry out what you want to do.

4. Let go of control

Sometimes we have this tendency to want to control everything. We want everything to be carefully outlined and followed, and if things do not go as planned, we freak out and worry. We think that if things do not go our way, everything will be a mess and chaos will follow. Sometimes because of worry, we even want to control the way people behave towards us or the way they think. But we all know this is impossible. We can never take control of everything, even our worries.

5. Change your perspective

Energy flows where you focus your attention. Understand that you can choose to focus on positive rather than negative thoughts. In fact, as you become more positive, you will be better able to create more positive outcomes. Always choose to be optimistic. Train your brain to be calm and composed and look at the positive side of things. The more positive you get, the more positive the results will be.

Conclusion

We have discussed extensively on the controversial truths we choose to ignore, we should accept the harsh truths of life and most importantly, not live like someone else or run after something which is not ours. We should spend our lives in trying to be a better person, in believing in ourselves and living in the present and not in any illusion.

It is not that we do not have the capacity to accept the truth. We choose not to accept it, and we hide behind the bar of our own logic and intelligence while the truth marches by and one day we come face to face with it. But what we need to understand is that accepting the truth gives us closure to our own questions and the sooner we accept them, the sooner we experience happiness in life.

Printed in Great Britain
by Amazon

48712148R00058